MW00907499

Success With

Reading
Tests

SCHOLASTIC

Editor: Ourania Papacharalambous
Educational consultant: Michael Priestley
Cover design by Tannaz Fassihi; cover illustration by Kevin Zimmer
Interior design by Michelle H. Kim
Interior illustrations by Doug Jones (spot art)

ISBN 978-1-338-79866-1
Scholastic Inc., 557 Broadway, New York, NY 10012
Copyright © 2022 Scholastic Inc.
All rights reserved. Printed in the U.S.A.
First printing, January 2022

1 2 3 4 5 6 7 8 9 10   40   29 28 27 26 25 24 23 22

INTRODUCTION

The Scholastic Success With Reading Tests series is designed to help you help students succeed on standardized tests. In this workbook for fifth graders, the 10 four-page tests are culled from the reading skills practice tests provided three times a year to *Scholastic News Edition 5* subscribers, with some new and revised material. By familiarizing students with the skills, language, and formats they will encounter on state and national tests, these practice tests will boost confidence and help raise scores.

The Reading Comprehension portion of the tests measures a student's ability to read and understand different types of prose. The tests contain passages of various lengths and about various subjects. Some of the questions require students to form an understanding based on information that is explicitly stated in the passage; others require forming an understanding based on information that is only implicit in the passage.

The questions supporting each test are specifically designed to review the following skills:

- **Find the Main Idea**
- **Identify Sequence**
- **Read for Detail**
- **Identify Cause and Effect**
- **Understand Vocabulary**
- **Recognize Author's Purpose**
- **Make Inferences**
- **Identify Fact and Opinion**

The Vocabulary portion of the tests measures a student's vocabulary and varies with each test. Some tests task students with identifying synonyms and antonyms; others require students to use context to choose a word that best completes a sentence.

Note that the tests in the second half of the book are slightly more difficult. These are designed to be given later in the school year.

In addition to helping students prepare for "real" tests, the practice tests in this workbook may be used as a diagnostic tool, to help you detect individual students' strengths and weaknesses, or as an instructional tool, for oral reading and discussion.

Keep in mind that our practice tests are just that—practice. These tests are not standardized. They should not be used to determine grade level, to compare one student's performance with that of others, or to evaluate teachers' abilities.

HOW TO USE AND ADMINISTER THE TESTS

Before administering each test, you may wish to review with students some basic information as well as helpful test-taking strategies, such as reading the questions before reading the passages.

- Establish a relaxed atmosphere. Explain to students that they will not be graded and that they are taking the test to practice for "real" tests down the road.

- Encourage students to do their best, but not to worry if they don't know all the answers.

- Provide each student with a sharpened pencil with a good eraser.

- Review the directions, then read the samples in each section and discuss the answers. Be sure to pay close attention to the directions in the vocabulary section on the last page of each test.

- To mimic the atmosphere of a real test, you may wish to set time limits. Students should be able to complete the reading comprehension section (the first three pages of each test) in 20 to 25 minutes. Allow an additional 10 minutes for the vocabulary portion on the last page of each test. Encourage students to work quickly and carefully and to keep track of the remaining time—just as they would in a real testing session.

- During the test, walk around the room and, as needed, guide students to:
    - make sure that they mark one answer circle for each question.
    - be sure to read the passages before marking answers.
    - use an eraser to make any changes to answers.
    - not copy the work of other students.

- If students are taking too much time with a particular question, tell them to eliminate the answer choices that are wrong first, then to choose the answer they think is the best choice from the remaining answers. (While "guessing" is not to be encouraged, encouraging students to mark an answer, even if they are not sure, will help them make use of whatever partial knowledge they may have.)

- Watch for students who stop working before they have done all the questions and encourage them to keep working.

- Encourage students to check their work after they have finished.

At the back of this book, you will find Tested Skills charts and an Answer Key for the 10 Practice Tests. The Tested Skills charts list the core standards and skills and the test questions that measure each. The charts may be helpful to you in determining what kinds of questions students answered incorrectly, what skills they may be having trouble with, and who may need further instruction in particular skills.

Reading Skills Practice Test 1
Reading Comprehension

Read each passage. Then, fill in the circle that best completes each sentence or answers each question.

SAMPLE

Have you ever seen someone on the beach with a sunburn? A sunburn can be quite painful. If the burn is really bad, the skin might blister and peel. Sunburn is caused by the sun's powerful ultraviolet (UV) rays. Wearing sunscreen can **shield** your skin from those damaging rays.

1 What is the main idea of this passage?
Ⓐ Ultraviolet rays cause sunburn.
Ⓑ Sunburn can cause fever.
Ⓒ Sunscreen makes skin peel.
Ⓓ It gets hot at the beach.

2 In this passage, the word **shield** means
Ⓐ burn.   Ⓒ protect.
Ⓑ lift.   Ⓓ open.

A. Animals depend on plants and other animals for food. The relationship among these animals and plants is called a food chain. The food chain keeps nature in balance. Here's how it works:

1. **Producers:** Plants and other organisms that provide food for animals make up the first link in a food chain.

2. **Herbivores:** These are animals that eat only plants. Called "prey," they are hunted by meat eaters.

3. **Carnivores:** These meat eaters feed on herbivores. They are also called "predators." When they die, their remains fertilize the ground and help plants grow.

1 What is the best title for this passage?
Ⓐ "Plant-Eating Animals"
Ⓑ "Understanding the Food Chain"
Ⓒ "Predators"
Ⓓ "Plants That Need Animals"

2 Animals that eat meat are called
Ⓐ herbivores.   Ⓒ prey.
Ⓑ producers.   Ⓓ carnivores.

3 You can guess from this passage that
Ⓐ herbivores are hungrier than carnivores.
Ⓑ herbivores are small animals.
Ⓒ carnivores eat lots of vegetables.
Ⓓ each link in the food chain is important.

B. In Greek mythology, Zeus and Hera were the leaders of the Greek gods. They were husband and wife. Hera sometimes became angry with Zeus when he spent too much time away from home.

Sometimes, Zeus went to the mountains to play with the forest creatures who lived there. Hera always chased after him because she thought Zeus was wasting time. But every time Hera entered the forest, a charming creature named Echo chatted with her and distracted her until Zeus had escaped.

When Hera figured out Echo had been tricking her, she was **furious**. "Your talk has made a fool of me!" she screamed. "From now on you will have nothing to say, except what others say to you first!"

From that day on, poor Echo could only repeat the last word of what others said.

1 This passage is mostly about
   Ⓐ Greek gods.   Ⓒ forests.
   Ⓑ Greece.   Ⓓ tricks.

2 You can guess from the passage that
   Ⓐ Zeus was tall and handsome.
   Ⓑ Echo lost her voice.
   Ⓒ Hera was very gentle.
   Ⓓ Echo lived in the forest.

3 In this passage, the word **furious** means
   Ⓐ angry.   Ⓒ foolish.
   Ⓑ happy.   Ⓓ tricky.

4 Zeus and Hera were
   Ⓐ soldiers.   Ⓒ married.
   Ⓑ forest creatures. Ⓓ human.

C. When you play a sport, do you feel that you must win—or else? The Youth Sports Institute in Michigan surveyed 26,000 boys and girls on this topic and found that many feel pushed to be the best.

Where does the pressure come from? Some kids put pressure on themselves, but many say that parents and coaches are also to blame.

They say these adults care only about the final score—not whether kids tried hard or had a good time.

1 What is the main idea of this passage?
   Ⓐ Fewer kids should play baseball.
   Ⓑ Youth sports are always fun.
   Ⓒ Many kids feel a lot of pressure to win at sports.
   Ⓓ Parents should be banned from going to kids' games.

2 Which of the statements is a *fact?*
   Ⓐ Sports pressure is the worst part of kids' sports.
   Ⓑ The Youth Sports Institute surveyed 26,000 kids.
   Ⓒ Winning is important.
   Ⓓ Coaches should not be allowed to pressure players.

3 The author wrote this passage to
   Ⓐ tell why baseball is good exercise.
   Ⓑ tell kids to quit playing sports.
   Ⓒ tell about the history of youth sports.
   Ⓓ tell about a problem in youth sports.

D. Wanda and Tina had been best friends for years. They did everything together. That's why Wanda was so surprised one day when Tina wouldn't talk to her. She had saved Tina a seat in the lunchroom, but when Tina came in, she went off and sat by herself.

Wanda didn't know what was wrong. Could Tina be mad at her? She thought about what she had done and said recently. Was Tina upset because Wanda had done better on the history test than she had? No, Tina didn't care about that kind of thing. She was happy that Wanda did well in school.

Wanda decided to find out what was the matter. She walked over to where Tina was sitting. "Tina," she said softly, "Is something wrong?"

Tina looked up, momentarily **perplexed**. Then she realized who it was. "Oh, hi, Wanda," she said. "Yes, something is wrong. My cat Zorro died today. I've been really sad. Thanks for asking. You're a true friend." Then she smiled. Wanda sat down next to her friend and gave her a big hug.

1 In this passage the word **perplexed** means

Ⓐ happy. Ⓒ bored.

Ⓑ intelligent. Ⓓ confused.

2 Why was Tina ignoring Wanda?

Ⓐ She was sad that her cat had died.

Ⓑ She was mad that Wanda had done well on the history test.

Ⓒ She didn't want to be Wanda's friend anymore.

Ⓓ She didn't want to share her lunch.

E. Falcons were dying. Air pollution was making the shells of their eggs too thin. When nesting mothers sat on the eggs, they would break. If something wasn't done, falcons would die off forever.

All across America, animals were dying. Gray wolves, brown pelicans, bald eagles, and others were all in danger of becoming extinct. So, in 1973, the United States government took action. It signed into law the Endangered Species Act.

This law gave the Fish and Wildlife Service the power to save endangered plants or animals. Any animal on the list would be protected by law from hunters or pollution.

In recent years, several animals and plants have been considered for de-listing. That means that they could be taken off the endangered-species list, and are no longer considered in danger of becoming extinct.

1 What happens to animals on the endangered species list?

Ⓐ They are protected by law from hunters and pollution.

Ⓑ They are kept in zoos to reproduce.

Ⓒ They begin dying off.

Ⓓ They get taken off after a year.

2 Why were the falcons dying?

Ⓐ They were being over-hunted.

Ⓑ Pollution was making the shells of their eggs too thin.

Ⓒ Gray wolves were eating them.

Ⓓ They had been on the endangered-species list for 25 years.

Vocabulary

Which Word Is Missing?

In each of the following paragraphs, a word is missing. First, read the paragraph. Then, find the missing word in the list of words beneath the paragraph. Fill in the circle next to the word that is missing.

Sample:

The car suddenly stopped in the middle of the road. It had run out of _____. The driver had forgotten to fill up the gas tank.

- (A) miles
- (C) water
- (B) fuel
- (D) popcorn

1 Some really large animals live on the plains of Africa. You might think the biggest ones would be the mightiest hunters, but that's not the case at all. Some of the world's biggest animals eat nothing but leaves, grasses, and shrubs. Instead of hunting other animals, these huge creatures _____ on plant life to survive.

- (A) dwell
- (C) grow
- (B) sit
- (D) graze

2 The largest plant eater of all is the African Elephant. In fact, the African elephant is the largest land _____ in the entire world! An adult elephant can weigh as much as 12,000 pounds. And a baby elephant is not exactly tiny: It can weigh up to 250 pounds at birth!

- (A) shark
- (C) mammal
- (B) soil
- (D) farmer

3 Another very large African plant eater is

the white rhinoceros. It is second in size only to the elephant. An adult male white rhino can weigh up to 8,000 pounds, or four _____.

- (A) pounds
- (C) ounces
- (B) tons
- (D) feet

4 The black rhino is a _____ of the white rhino. Although the two are kin, the black rhino doesn't get nearly as large. At 3,000 pounds, though, the adult male black rhino is still pretty big. Both rhinos are very good at using their horns to break off tree branches for dinner.

- (A) relative
- (C) friend
- (B) neighbor
- (D) killer

5 Another large African plant eater is the hippopotamus. An adult male hippo can weigh up to four tons. Despite a hippo's large size, they only eat about 88 pounds of food a day. Another interesting fact is that hippos have sensitive skin that can get dry. To keep their skin _____, they hang out in rivers.

- (A) rough
- (C) brown
- (B) moist
- (D) clean

Reading Skills Practice Test 2
Reading Comprehension

Read each passage. Then, fill in the circle that best completes each sentence or answers each question.

SAMPLE

How cool can glasses get? Try these on. New experimental glasses plug into the brain and help blind people "see" again. A tiny video camera and a distance-measuring machine sit on the lenses. The camera takes a picture and sends the image into a computer worn on a belt. The computer hooks up to the brain through wires and sends signals to the part of the brain that controls sight.

1 What is the best title for this passage?
Ⓐ "The Power of Cameras"
Ⓑ "Helping People See"
Ⓒ "Cameras and Computers"
Ⓓ "Being Blind"

A. What do you think of when you hear the word *anaconda*? If you're like many people, you think of a giant snake that lives in the Amazon and that eats people. But you would be wrong.

Although anacondas do live in the Amazon region of South America, they do not eat humans. They do eat animals as large as deer, however. An anaconda kills its prey by giving it a deadly squeeze. This **lethal** hug cuts off the victim's air supply and blood flow.

Scientists still need to find out more about these powerful snakes. For instance, no one really knows how they reproduce.

1 How does an anaconda kill its prey?
Ⓐ by squeezing it
Ⓑ by biting it
Ⓒ by drowning it
Ⓓ by eating it

2 In this passage, the word **lethal** means
Ⓐ friendly.   Ⓒ tight.
Ⓑ painful.   Ⓓ deadly.

3 The purpose of this passage is to
Ⓐ persuade you that anacondas are beautiful.
Ⓑ inform you about anacondas in general.
Ⓒ warn you that anacondas are dangerous.
Ⓓ amaze you with the size of anacondas.

B. Shelley Langdon couldn't wait for summer vacation to start. This year her family was renting a beach house on the Outer Banks in North Carolina. Shelley had always heard that these barrier islands were beautiful, but she'd never been there.

To get to the beach house, the Langdons drove for hours. Finally, they crossed a bridge. When Shelley's dad came off the bridge and made a right, Shelley was amazed. She could see water on both sides of her. One side was full of boats. On the other side waves crashed against the sand.

The Langdon's house, like all the others near it, was on stilts. A wooden walkway led down from the deck to the beach. Shelley hurriedly pulled on her bathing suit and ran to the water. There, she was in for a surprise! Out beyond the breakers were two porpoises, playing in the waves!

1 Based on this passage, which of the following statements might be true?
Ⓐ North Carolina is not a coastal state.
Ⓑ Shelley was very excited about her beach vacation.
Ⓒ Shelley's parents don't like the beach very much.
Ⓓ The Langdons live very near the Outer Banks.

2 Why was Shelley surprised?
Ⓐ The beach house was on stilts.
Ⓑ There were porpoises playing in the waves.
Ⓒ It was a long drive to the beach.
Ⓓ The Outer Banks were very ugly.

C. These days almost everyone knows that olive oil is good for you. But what most people may not know is that olive oil is used for more than just food. People make soap out of it, polish diamonds with it, and burn it for light. In ancient times, boiling olive oil was even used as a weapon of war.

Traditionally, olive oil was mainly used by people in Mediterranean countries. But these days, more and more people all over the world are discovering that olive oil may be the best oil for cooking. In the United States, people use five times more olive oil today than they did 20 years ago.

Ninety-five percent of the world's olive oil is still produced in Mediterranean countries. Spain leads the list in producing the most olive oil, followed by Italy, Greece, Tunisia, and Turkey.

1 Which of these is an *opinion*?
Ⓐ Olive oil is used for a lot more than just food.
Ⓑ Olive oil may be the best oil for cooking.
Ⓒ Americans use five times more olive oil than they did 20 years ago.
Ⓓ Ninety-nine percent of the world's olive oil is produced in Mediterranean countries.

2 The biggest producer of olive oil is
Ⓐ Italy.   Ⓒ Greece.
Ⓑ Turkey.   Ⓓ Spain.

D. Can you imagine being trapped on a ship for nine months? That's what happened to an expedition led by Sir Ernest Shackleton.

Shackleton and his crew were trying to reach Antarctica when their ship, the Endurance, became trapped in polar ice on January 18, 1915. For nine months they waited for the ice to break up. Finally, in October, the crew abandoned the ship and set sail in three rickety lifeboats.

Hundreds of miles later, the men reached **barren** Elephant Island. Shackleton realized that they could not survive there. So, he and five other men set out in one of the lifeboats for an 800-mile journey to South Georgia Island. They knew that there were people there who could help them.

Seventeen days later, the men arrived. Shackleton took a ship back to Elephant Island and rescued the rest of his crew. Amazingly, everyone was still alive. After over a year of cold and starvation, the men from the Endurance were safe at last.

1 What happened after Shackleton arrived at South Georgia Island?
- Ⓐ He rescued the rest of his crew.
- Ⓑ He set sail in a lifeboat.
- Ⓒ The Endurance got trapped in the ice.
- Ⓓ The crew waited nine months for the ice to break up.

2 In this passage, the word **barren** means
- Ⓐ large.
- Ⓒ mountainous.
- Ⓑ lifeless.
- Ⓓ forested.

E. Hunger is not just a problem for the poor countries of the world. Even in the United States, there are plenty of people who don't get enough to eat. Some of these people are children. In 2017, 1 in 6 (12.5 million) children in the United States lived in food-insecure households.

Hunger can have much more serious **consequences** than just a growling stomach. Children dealing with hunger pains have trouble paying attention in school. They don't have the energy to run around on the playground during recess. And not getting enough to eat for a long time can slow a kid's growth and brain development.

What can you do to help stop hunger? A good place to start is giving time to programs that feed hungry children. Try volunteering at a soup kitchen in your community. One volunteer had this to say about helping to feed kids in his hometown: "It makes me really happy to see the kids eat. All kids have the right to eat."

1 In this passage, the word **consequences** means
- Ⓐ effects.
- Ⓒ illnesses.
- Ⓑ problems.
- Ⓓ losses.

2 According to the passage, which of the following is not a consequence of hunger?
- Ⓐ a lack of energy
- Ⓑ bad skin
- Ⓒ slow growth
- Ⓓ trouble paying attention

Vocabulary

Synonyms

Read the underlined word in each phrase.
Mark the word below it that has the same
(or close to the same) meaning.

Sample:

quite <u>reluctant</u>
- Ⓐ eager
- Ⓑ unwilling
- Ⓒ unhappy
- Ⓓ surprised

1 <u>bestow</u> this
- Ⓐ give
- Ⓑ take
- Ⓒ tow
- Ⓓ allow

2 with <u>liberty</u>
- Ⓐ triumph
- Ⓑ faith
- Ⓒ freedom
- Ⓓ caution

3 very <u>evident</u>
- Ⓐ unlikely
- Ⓑ obvious
- Ⓒ wise
- Ⓓ unclear

4 <u>gape</u> at
- Ⓐ sneer
- Ⓑ squint
- Ⓒ smile
- Ⓓ stare

5 <u>minor</u> problems
- Ⓐ small
- Ⓑ large
- Ⓒ difficult
- Ⓓ easy

6 <u>swivel</u> around
- Ⓐ look
- Ⓑ turn
- Ⓒ fly
- Ⓓ float

7 <u>contribute</u> aid
- Ⓐ purchase
- Ⓑ donate
- Ⓒ return
- Ⓓ accept

Antonyms

Read the underlined word in each phrase.
Mark the word below it that means the
opposite or nearly the opposite.

Sample:

<u>idle</u> worker
- Ⓐ hard
- Ⓑ lazy
- Ⓒ busy
- Ⓓ retired

1 feel <u>panic</u>
- Ⓐ calm
- Ⓑ upset
- Ⓒ disgust
- Ⓓ content

2 <u>spectacular</u> event
- Ⓐ amazing
- Ⓑ joyful
- Ⓒ tragic
- Ⓓ ordinary

3 <u>smug</u> expression
- Ⓐ delighted
- Ⓑ self-satisfied
- Ⓒ calm
- Ⓓ unsure

4 <u>wary</u> glance
- Ⓐ carefree
- Ⓑ cautious
- Ⓒ timid
- Ⓓ quick

5 <u>inferior</u> brand
- Ⓐ exterior
- Ⓑ popular
- Ⓒ superior
- Ⓓ expensive

6 <u>carefree</u> attitude
- Ⓐ unbelievable
- Ⓑ laughing
- Ⓒ happy
- Ⓓ serious

7 <u>clammy</u> grip
- Ⓐ cold
- Ⓑ firm
- Ⓒ icy and wet
- Ⓓ dry

Reading Skills Practice Test 3
Reading Comprehension

Read each passage. Then, fill in the circle that best completes each sentence or answers each question.

SAMPLE

Everyone knows that spinach is good for you. But who knew that it was first used as a treat for cats? That's right, cats. Spinach was originally grown in ancient Persia. The ancient Persians used it to satisfy the finicky appetites of their cats. Soon people began to love it, too. Today, people all over the world cook with this versatile vegetable.

1 What is the best title for this passage?
Ⓐ "Green Vegetables"
Ⓑ "Persian cats"
Ⓒ "Versatile Vegetables"
Ⓓ "Spinach"

2 Why was spinach originally grown?
Ⓐ because people loved it
Ⓑ because cats loved it
Ⓒ because it's healthy
Ⓓ because it's versatile

A. You're standing by the locker and hear two kids yelling. Their voices get louder and louder. You just know a fight is going to break out. How do you stop it?

If you're a peer mediator, you know how to handle the problem. Peer mediators are students who are trained to help solve arguments before they turn into fights.

When a disagreement breaks out, two peer mediators step in. They listen to both sides and ask both kids how they want to see the problem **resolved**. If both kids agree to the terms, the mediators draw up a contract that each kid signs.

As long as the kids stick to the agreement, everyone wins. Many schools have had less fighting and fewer suspensions since they started using peer mediation.

1 What are peer mediators?
Ⓐ teachers who have been trained to stop fights
Ⓑ students who have been trained to solve arguments
Ⓒ students who fight a lot
Ⓓ students who get suspended a lot

2 In this passage, the word **resolved** means
Ⓐ worked out. Ⓒ ignored.
Ⓑ reported. Ⓓ forgotten about.

3 The purpose of this passage is to
Ⓐ persuade you that peer mediators don't work.
Ⓑ inform you about peer mediators.
Ⓒ warn you that fighting is a problem in schools.
Ⓓ amuse you with school-fight stories.

Name _____   Date _____

B. You may already know that the Taj Mahal is in India. You may know that many people consider it one of the world's most beautiful buildings. But did you know that this marble masterpiece was built for love?

Emperor Shah Jahan built the Taj Mahal to honor his wife, Mumtaz Mahal. She died in 1629. They had been married for 17 years. The emperor was heartbroken. He decided to honor her with a monument.

The Taj Mahal took more than 20 years to build. Twenty thousand people worked on it. Experts were brought in from as far away as Europe. The building was finished in 1653. It quickly became famous. For more than 300 years, people have flocked to see this stunning monument to love.

1 Which of these is an *opinion*?
   Ⓐ Twenty thousand people worked on the Taj Mahal.
   Ⓑ The building was finished in 1653.
   Ⓒ The Taj Mahal is the most beautiful building in the world.
   Ⓓ Shah Jahan was heartbroken when his wife, Mumtaz Mahal, died.

2 How long were Shah Jahan and Mumtaz Mahal married?
   Ⓐ 12 years   Ⓒ 20 years
   Ⓑ 17 years   Ⓓ 30 years

3 What is a good title for this passage?
   Ⓐ "Great Buildings of the World"
   Ⓑ "Built for Love"
   Ⓒ "Indian Emperors"
   Ⓓ "Mumtaz Mahal"

C. There are four things you need to know about Malik Jones. **1.** He's in my homeroom. **2.** He plays baseball. **3.** He gets good grades. **4.** He's the most annoying person who ever lived.

Why would a person always stare at me, or talk about my hair, unless it was to annoy me? No matter where I am, Malik is sure to walk by and make a comment. Everyone else thinks it's funny. I just think it's annoying.

So, the other day, I finally confronted him. "Malik Jones," I said, "What makes you think you can always talk about my hair?" He looked startled for a minute. "Well," he finally said, "I like your hair. That's why I'm always talking about it. I think it's beautiful." Did I mention that Malik Jones is one of the nicest guys who ever lived?

1 Which of these is an *opinion*?
   Ⓐ Malik plays baseball.
   Ⓑ Malik gets good grades.
   Ⓒ Malik is in the speaker's homeroom.
   Ⓓ Malik is the most annoying person who ever lived.

2 How would you describe the speaker?
   Ⓐ shy   Ⓒ quiet
   Ⓑ opinionated   Ⓓ boring

3 You can conclude from this passage's ending that
   Ⓐ the speaker still finds Malik annoying.
   Ⓑ the speaker likes Malik now.
   Ⓒ Malik doesn't like the speaker.
   Ⓓ Malik and the speaker are related.

D. Eighteen-year-old Billy Campbell was riding harder than he had ever ridden before. His horse was exhausted. Its chest and sides were full of sweat. Campbell hated to push the horse any faster. But he had to make it to the next station.

Billy Campbell was a rider on the Pony Express. The Pony Express was the nation's first "express" mail delivery service. It was set up in 1860 to carry mail from Missouri to California.

The Pony Express riders were all young men like Billy Campbell. They had to be light of weight and excellent horsemen. Each rider galloped at least 75 miles a day, changing horses several times.

The Pony Express was a success. It got mail to California faster than ever before. Unfortunately, it was also short-lived. A new coast-to-coast telegraph system soon made the Pony Express unnecessary. It was shut down a year and a half after it began.

1 Why did the Pony Express go out of business?
Ⓐ The telegraph replaced it.
Ⓑ It was too dangerous.
Ⓒ It ran out of horses.
Ⓓ It wasn't a success.

2 The Pony Express carried mail from
Ⓐ Ohio to Texas.
Ⓑ Colorado to Oregon.
Ⓒ Boston to Cleveland.
Ⓓ Missouri to California.

E. Dear Travel Section Editor,
Last week's story on Yellowstone and Yosemite national parks was terrific. I would like to make a suggestion for a future article. How about a story on smaller, less well-known parks and monuments? I can suggest three.

The Craters of the Moon National Monument in Idaho contains some of the country's strangest scenery. Its lava flows, volcanic cones, and ice caves will astound visitors. Another of my favorite parks is Indiana Dunes National Park. You might not expect big sand dunes in Indiana, but there they are! Visitors can swim, hike, and climb at Lake Michigan's shore. Finally, for an educational trip, there's Women's Rights National Historical Park. Located in Seneca Falls, New York, it contains the site of the first Women's Rights Convention. Visitors learn about the struggle of women to achieve voting rights.

Sincerely,
A National Park Fan

1 The letter's main idea is that
Ⓐ some smaller national parks are interesting.
Ⓑ tourists like parks.
Ⓒ the travel section is boring.
Ⓓ parks have strange scenery.

2 Seneca Falls is the site of
Ⓐ Yosemite.
Ⓑ Yellowstone.
Ⓒ Craters of the Moon.
Ⓓ the Women's Rights National Historical Park.

Vocabulary

Synonyms

Read the underlined word in each phrase.
Mark the word below it that has the same
(or close to the same) meaning.

Sample:
comic situation
- Ⓐ sad
- Ⓑ formal
- Ⓒ tense
- Ⓓ funny

1 enable him
- Ⓐ follow
- Ⓑ imitate
- Ⓒ allow
- Ⓓ remind

2 a weird feeling
- Ⓐ bad
- Ⓑ good
- Ⓒ strange
- Ⓓ happy

3 a throng of people
- Ⓐ crowd
- Ⓑ line
- Ⓒ wall
- Ⓓ scattering

4 a funny notion
- Ⓐ joke
- Ⓑ face
- Ⓒ idea
- Ⓓ game

5 forthright talk
- Ⓐ loud
- Ⓑ scared
- Ⓒ smooth
- Ⓓ direct

6 murky water
- Ⓐ clear
- Ⓑ rough
- Ⓒ muddy
- Ⓓ deep

7 luxurious furnishings
- Ⓐ uncomfortable
- Ⓑ attractive
- Ⓒ expensive
- Ⓓ cheap

Antonyms

Read the underlined word in each phrase.
Mark the word below it that means the
opposite or nearly the opposite.

Sample:
damp room
- Ⓐ wet
- Ⓑ dry
- Ⓒ large
- Ⓓ tiny

1 noisy party
- Ⓐ quiet
- Ⓑ loud
- Ⓒ crowded
- Ⓓ empty

2 reckless behavior
- Ⓐ careless
- Ⓑ careful
- Ⓒ proud
- Ⓓ humble

3 reject the answer
- Ⓐ turn down
- Ⓑ withhold
- Ⓒ shout
- Ⓓ accept

4 coarse crumbs
- Ⓐ cake
- Ⓑ bread
- Ⓒ fine
- Ⓓ chunky

5 scaly skin
- Ⓐ smooth
- Ⓑ dry
- Ⓒ dark
- Ⓓ light

6 distinguished visitor
- Ⓐ important
- Ⓑ unimportant
- Ⓒ pretentious
- Ⓓ disliked

7 offensive odor
- Ⓐ nasty
- Ⓑ strong
- Ⓒ pleasing
- Ⓓ sweet

Reading Skills Practice Test 4
Reading Comprehension

Read each passage. Then, fill in the circle that best completes each sentence or answers each question.

SAMPLE

When it comes to jumping, you might think frogs or kangaroos are the champs. Wrong! Grasshoppers have the greatest jumping ability of all animals in relation to their size. Grasshoppers can jump two feet high and four feet forward. That's equal to a human jumping over a tall building.

1 The best title for this passage is
Ⓐ "Grasshoppers: Super Jumpers."
Ⓑ "Frogs, Kangaroos, and Grasshoppers."
Ⓒ "When Humans Jump Over Buildings."
Ⓓ "Grasshoppers Are Better Than People."

2 This author's point about grasshoppers is that
Ⓐ they can jump over buildings.
Ⓑ they can grow to be as tall as humans.
Ⓒ they can jump very high for how small they are.
Ⓓ they jump on only two feet.

A. Morgan White's lifelong dream was to compete in gymnastics in the Olympics. She fell in love with gymnastics at age five, after watching a competition on TV. She became a top American gymnast.

Morgan's favorite event was the uneven bars. In it, a gymnast must move from a high bar to a low one with different swinging motions. Morgan was so good at it that there's a gymnastic move named after her. The move, called "The White," involves a handstand and twist on the bars.

Becoming so good meant making many sacrifices. "All the girls in my group—we couldn't do after-school activities," said Morgan. "I couldn't stay up late because

I had to get up for a workout early in the morning." But, she said, all the sacrifices were worth it.

1 What is the best title for this passage?
Ⓐ "No After-School Activities"
Ⓑ "The Olympics"
Ⓒ "Gymnastics"
Ⓓ "Morgan White: Gymnast"

2 From this passage, you can conclude that
Ⓐ Morgan worked very hard at gymnastics.
Ⓑ Morgan watched a lot of TV.
Ⓒ Boys do not do gymnastics.
Ⓓ Morgan only liked the uneven bars.

B. Karla Pierce was enjoying a springtime family barbecue in Skowhegan, Maine, when it happened. Her friend's dog, Tucker, accidentally fell into a nearby stream. The stream was thick with melted snow, and Tucker was heading straight for a dam.

Karla knew she had to be calm, stay focused, and act fast. She ran through some hay fields to the edge of the stream. Meanwhile, a few of the adults at the barbecue drove to the stream to reach Tucker before he got to the dam.

Karla got to the edge of the stream first. She hooked her foot around a small tree and hung her body over the water to try and reach the dog. Kara could see that Tucker was fighting the water's **current**, or its movement, and was hitting some rocks. But Karla was able to grab Tucker by the front paws and, with some true muscle, pull him out of the stream.

1 This passage is mostly about
  Ⓐ how Karla saved her friend's dog, Tucker.
  Ⓑ why water currents can be dangerous.
  Ⓒ swimming dogs.
  Ⓓ Karla Pierce's friends and family.

2 Which is a *fact*?
  Ⓐ A dog should be kept on a leash.
  Ⓑ Karla Pierce was brave to save her friend's dog.
  Ⓒ A water's **current** means the speed of its movement.
  Ⓓ Tucker was a lucky dog.

C. Bike helmets are made of hard foam that absorbs the force of a fall. But if a helmet does not fit, it will not protect the head properly. To make sure your helmet has the right fit, follow these steps:
- Try on helmets. A helmet shouldn't be too tight, but it shouldn't be so big that it **jostles** back and forth.
- Stick soft adhesive pads on the inside of the helmet to make it fit just right.
- Keep the front of your helmet just above your eyebrows when you ride.
- Make sure the chin strap fits securely under your chin.

1 What is the best title for this passage?
  Ⓐ "Helmets: Get the Perfect Fit"
  Ⓑ "Biking: Rules of the Road"
  Ⓒ "Buying a Bike"
  Ⓓ "Bike Helmet Laws"

2 In this passage, the word **jostles** means
  Ⓐ teases.   Ⓒ rides.
  Ⓑ sticks.   Ⓓ moves.

3 This passage is best for someone who
  Ⓐ rides on busy streets.
  Ⓑ has an old helmet.
  Ⓒ is buying a new helmet.
  Ⓓ rides a mountain bike.

4 You would probably find this passage in
  Ⓐ a book about running.
  Ⓑ an article about foam.
  Ⓒ a pamphlet about safety while riding a bicycle.
  Ⓓ a magazine about motorcycles.

D. In New York State, some pesky critters may be playing a deadly trick on a Halloween treat. Scientists think that microbes, or bugs so small that they can't be seen without a microscope, are to blame for a strange disease cropping up in some pumpkin patches.

The disease clogs tiny vessels, or tubes, inside the pumpkins. These tubes carry water and nutrients. When the vessels are blocked, pumpkins can't get the **nourishment** they need. So, they starve. Infected pumpkins lose their bright-orange color and eventually rot.

The mysterious disease has also been spotted in New York squash and cucumbers. But that doesn't mean people should start worrying about a vegetable shortage. The sick veggies are only a small percentage of the pumpkin, squash, and cucumber crops. So those who were secretly hoping for a few vegetable-free meals better get ready for second helpings instead.

1 In this passage, the word **nourishment** means
(A) bugs.
(B) care.
(C) sunlight.
(D) food and water.

2 How does the disease kill pumpkins?
(A) It clogs vessels inside the pumpkins.
(B) It clogs the pumpkin plants' roots.
(C) It makes the pumpkins lose their orange color.
(D) It makes the pumpkins stop growing.

E. Have you ever tried to write a poem? It's easier than you might think. Poems are a lot like song lyrics. A good poem reveals an honest feeling about something. Follow these steps to write a poem.

1. First, choose your topic. What would you like your poem to be about? Your poem will be more powerful if you choose a topic you feel strongly about.

2. Now freewrite for five minutes about your topic. Then, go back and read it. Do any words or phrases stand out? Circle these to use in your poem.

3. Write your poem. Remember, a poem doesn't have to rhyme. It doesn't have to use sentences. But it should show your feelings about the topic. And it should sound nice to you.

4. Have a friend read your poem aloud to you. Do you like the way it sounds? If not, go back and rewrite the parts you don't like.

5. Enjoy your poem. Read it to others and to yourself. Post it somewhere if you want.

1 To write a poem, what should you do first?
(A) Freewrite.
(B) Have a friend read a poem aloud.
(C) Choose a topic.
(D) Rewrite.

2 In which step of poetry writing do you rewrite?
(A) 1
(B) 2
(C) 4
(D) 5

Vocabulary

Synonyms

Read the underlined word in each phrase. Mark the word below it that has the same (or close to the same) meaning.

Sample:

wool and cotton <u>blend</u>
- Ⓐ fabric
- Ⓒ mix
- Ⓑ material
- Ⓓ layer

1 I <u>resemble</u> him
- Ⓐ look like
- Ⓒ hate
- Ⓑ resent
- Ⓓ watch

2 a big <u>guffaw</u>
- Ⓐ scream
- Ⓒ laugh
- Ⓑ yell
- Ⓓ cry

3 <u>devour</u> the food
- Ⓐ throw out
- Ⓒ cook
- Ⓑ eat
- Ⓓ feed

4 <u>possess</u> a book
- Ⓐ own
- Ⓒ carry
- Ⓑ lend
- Ⓓ read

5 a great <u>location</u>
- Ⓐ job
- Ⓒ scene
- Ⓑ place
- Ⓓ train

6 <u>capable</u> hands
- Ⓐ able
- Ⓒ clumsy
- Ⓑ unable
- Ⓓ fast

7 looking for <u>insight</u>
- Ⓐ contentment
- Ⓒ courtesy
- Ⓑ understanding
- Ⓓ forgiveness

Antonyms

Read the underlined word in each phrase. Mark the word below it that means the opposite or nearly the opposite.

Sample:

I <u>adore</u> her
- Ⓐ love
- Ⓒ like
- Ⓑ hate
- Ⓓ envy

1 a <u>wintry</u> day
- Ⓐ cold
- Ⓒ long
- Ⓑ warm
- Ⓓ tiring

2 <u>flammable</u> cloth
- Ⓐ aflame
- Ⓒ fireproof
- Ⓑ flimsy
- Ⓓ stiff

3 <u>embrace</u> an idea
- Ⓐ support
- Ⓒ dislike
- Ⓑ learn
- Ⓓ reject

4 <u>overjoyed</u> expression
- Ⓐ unhappy
- Ⓒ reserved
- Ⓑ beaming
- Ⓓ guarded

5 <u>classic</u> movie
- Ⓐ long
- Ⓒ short
- Ⓑ old
- Ⓓ new

6 <u>considerable</u> amount
- Ⓐ strange
- Ⓒ small
- Ⓑ expensive
- Ⓓ large

7 beg to <u>differ</u>
- Ⓐ digest
- Ⓒ agree
- Ⓑ defer
- Ⓓ assume

Name _____   Date _____

Reading Skills Practice Test 5
Reading Comprehension

Read each passage. Then, fill in the circle that best completes each sentence or answers each question.

SAMPLE

Ever wonder how much TV kids like you watch? Research shows that most American children watch three to five hours of TV every day. That's a lot. Is watching so much TV good or bad for kids?

Experts don't think watching TV is bad. They say that there are a lot of good shows for children. But they think it's important for kids to have better TV habits. Experts feel children should only watch one or two hours of TV a day.

1 According to the passage, how much TV do most kids watch?
Ⓐ half an hour a day
Ⓑ one or two hours a day
Ⓒ three to five hours a day
Ⓓ more than five hours a day

2 What is the main idea of this passage?
Ⓐ Kids don't watch enough TV.
Ⓑ Kids should watch one hour of TV a day.
Ⓒ Kids watch five hours of TV a day.
Ⓓ Kids should have better TV habits.

A. When gum gets stuck in your hair, it can be an icky, sticky mess. Here are two good ways to get the gum out.

• The quickest way is to cut the gum out of your hair. However, this may not be the best way if you care a lot about your hairstyle. Your hair may end up looking strange, and it may take a while to grow back to normal.

• Another good way is to ease it out with some sort of oil. Try cooking oil or peanut butter. Just put a small amount of the oil or peanut butter in your hair and **knead** the gum between your fingers to soften it. As the gum softens, pull it out gently and slowly.

1 What is the best title for this passage?
Ⓐ "The Perks of Peanut Butter"
Ⓑ "Getting the Gum Out"
Ⓒ "Horrible Hairstyles"
Ⓓ "Growing Out Your Hair"

2 In this passage, the word **knead** means
Ⓐ need.   Ⓒ press gently.
Ⓑ want.   Ⓓ punch hard.

3 What is the similarity between the two ways of getting gum out of your hair?
Ⓐ They both work.
Ⓑ They both ruin your hairstyle.
Ⓒ They both use peanut butter.
Ⓓ They both use scissors.

B. The next time you cool off with an ice-cold Popsicle, you can thank Frank Epperson. He was just 11 years old when he came up with this famous frozen treat. Here is what happened.

In 1905, young Frank mixed together some powdered soda pop to drink. He left the cup on the back porch overnight with the stirring stick still in it.

When Frank went out to the porch the next morning, he found a stick of frozen soda water. He brought it to school that day. Soon, he was selling his creation to friends.

The rest, as they say, is history. When Frank grew up, he patented his invention and named it the Popsicle. By 1928, more than 60 million Popsicles had been sold.

1 From this passage, you can guess that
Ⓐ Frank didn't like soda pop.
Ⓑ it was very cold the night Frank left his soda pop out.
Ⓒ Frank's friends thought the frozen soda pop tasted awful.
Ⓓ Frank's mother is responsible for the invention of Popsicles.

2 The purpose of this passage is to
Ⓐ inform you about the invention of Popsicles.
Ⓑ entertain you with Frank's story.
Ⓒ persuade you that Popsicles are delicious.
Ⓓ warn you that Popsicles are bad.

C. Imagine a wall of water as high as a 12-story building. What if that wall hit the coast of the United States? Some scientists think this could happen. They think the Northwest U.S. could be hit by this giant wave, called a tsunami (soo-nah-mee). This area could be threatened because it is across the ocean from the countries of eastern and southeastern Asia. That's where earthquakes create the largest tsunamis.

That's why scientists are testing a new machine. The machine will warn people about these waves—before they hit. When people don't know that a tsunami is coming, it can be deadly. For instance, a monster wave once hit the island of New Guinea and killed 2,200 people.

It is hoped that machines placed on the ocean floor will be able to measure the size of the waves. People will then know when they have to **flee** the coast because a big wave is on the way!

1 In this passage, the word **flee** means
Ⓐ run away.   Ⓒ destroy.
Ⓑ move toward.   Ⓓ protect.

2 How are scientists hoping to protect people against tsunamis?
Ⓐ by preventing tsunamis from happening
Ⓑ by using a machine that will warn people about tsunamis
Ⓒ by keeping people from living in the Northwest
Ⓓ by making the tsunamis into smaller

D. There were once two neighbors named Chen and Li. Chen was a rich man, but very unhappy. He worried about money constantly. Li was poor, but happy. He had few worries. Each night, Li's house was filled with laughing and singing.

One day, Chen invited Li to his house. "I am giving you 500 silver pieces to start your own business," he announced. "Even though you will become rich, do not pay me back." Li was shocked. He did not want to be rich. He knew that money caused worry. But he thanked Chen for his generosity and went home.

For the next few nights, there was no joy at Li's house. Li could not stop worrying about how to use the money. He could hardly sleep.

Finally, after several days, Li returned to Chen's house. He gave the money back and immediately felt relieved. He went home and ate dinner. He slept soundly the whole night through. And the next night, Li's house was filled with laughing and singing again.

1 What is Li's problem in this passage?
Ⓐ He doesn't have enough money.
Ⓑ He is not very happy.
Ⓒ He doesn't like to sleep or eat.
Ⓓ He's given what he doesn't want.

2 How does Li solve his problem?
Ⓐ He makes a lot of money.
Ⓑ He sings and laughs.
Ⓒ He sleeps late and eats a lot.
Ⓓ He gives the money back.

E. Mosquito bites are not just itchy and annoying. Now, in the United States, a rare kind of virus carried by certain mosquitoes may cause serious illness. In some extreme cases, it may even lead to death.

People first learned about this new virus in the summer of 1999 It was caused by the bites of certain mosquitoes. Experts believe these mosquitoes carry a form of the West Nile virus. Before 1999, this dangerous virus had never been found in the United States.

Most people infected with West Nile virus have no symptoms. Some, however, do get a fever and a headache. And some fall seriously ill. They have to be hospitalized.

The best defense against the West Nile virus is preventing mosquito bites. What's the best protection from these insects? Wear long-sleeved shirts and long pants. And keep the insect repellent close at hand!

1 What is the best title for this passage?
Ⓐ "The West Nile Virus"
Ⓑ "How to Treat Mosquito Bites"
Ⓒ "Annoying Insects"
Ⓓ "Protecting Yourself From Bites"

2 Which of the following is an *opinion*?
Ⓐ Some mosquitoes carry a dangerous virus.
Ⓑ Many people infected with West Nile virus have no symptoms.
Ⓒ Mosquito bites are so itchy and annoying.
Ⓓ Preventing mosquito bites helps prevent West Nile virus.

Vocabulary

Which Word Is Missing?

In each of the following paragraphs, a word is missing. First, read each paragraph. Then, choose the missing word from the list beneath the paragraph. Fill in the circle next to the word that is missing.

Sample:

Last night, Shawn's parents dragged him to the world's most boring movie. He sat in his seat, waiting for it to be over, but the film seemed _____.

Ⓐ fascinating   Ⓒ terrible

Ⓑ endless   Ⓓ brief

1 When Ayesha first hurt her wrist, she was in _____. The pain was unbearable.

Ⓐ ecstasy   Ⓒ mourning

Ⓑ denial   Ⓓ agony

2 Fortunately, it wasn't broken. "I could have _____ worse," she said to herself.

Ⓐ fared   Ⓒ expanded

Ⓑ ranged   Ⓓ read

3 She did, however, have to wear a cast for two weeks. She knew she could _____. After all, two weeks wasn't very long.

Ⓐ cry   Ⓒ survive

Ⓑ consent   Ⓓ grieve

4 Her friends all signed her cast. They used _____ colors so the signatures would stand out.

Ⓐ subtle   Ⓒ faint

Ⓑ large   Ⓓ vivid

5 When the cast came off, Ayesha was a little _____. It had become such a part of herself, she almost wanted it back.

Ⓐ wistful   Ⓒ eager

Ⓑ dreary   Ⓓ grateful

6 Most people think it's _____ to have soup for dessert. But I don't. I think it's perfectly normal.

Ⓐ ordinary   Ⓒ exciting

Ⓑ peculiar   Ⓓ irritating

7 I don't like sweets that much. But I do want something _____ after dinner. For me, soup fits the bill.

Ⓐ enjoyable   Ⓒ bitter

Ⓑ tasteless   Ⓓ elaborate

8 The appearance of a bowl of _____ soup always makes me happy. My nose fills with delicious aromas.

Ⓐ ordinary   Ⓒ greasy

Ⓑ murky   Ⓓ fragrant

9 Sometimes my friends can't help but _____ when my dad places a big bowl of steaming chowder in front of me—especially when they're having chocolate cake!

Ⓐ grandstand   Ⓒ snicker

Ⓑ babble   Ⓓ rejoice

Reading Skills Practice Test 6
Reading Comprehension

Read each passage. Then, fill in the circle that best completes each sentence or answers each question.

SAMPLE

Italy's Leaning Tower of Pisa was never straight. It started leaning before workers finished building it in the mid-1300s. Despite its **precarious** perch, the tower has maintained its tilt for 800 years. But all is not well with the tilting tower. These days, officials are worried that the eight-story tower might collapse.

1 The word **precarious** means
Ⓐ settled.   Ⓒ hilly.
Ⓑ risky.   Ⓓ previous.

2 Why are officials worried about the tower?
Ⓐ They are afraid it might collapse.
Ⓑ They think the tower is too old.
Ⓒ Workers never finished building it in the 1300s.
Ⓓ The town of Pisa was hit by an earthquake recently.

A. Have you ever heard a haiku? A haiku is a type of short poem that developed in Japan. Each haiku has only three lines and 17 syllables. The first and last lines have five syllables each. The second line has seven syllables.

Because of its small size, a haiku doesn't express long, complicated ideas. Usually, it simply tries to capture a single moment in time. Still, haiku is a very powerful form of poetry. Often, the subject is nature.

Although haiku developed years ago, the form is still popular in modern Japan. Many people make a hobby of composing haiku. Haiku clubs and magazines are also very popular.

1 How many syllables does a haiku contain?
Ⓐ 5   Ⓒ 15
Ⓑ 7   Ⓓ 17

2 You can conclude from this passage that
Ⓐ haikus are not as popular as they were in the past.
Ⓑ every haiku contains images from nature.
Ⓒ long poems are more interesting.
Ⓓ haiku was developed in Japan.

B.   The *Tyrannosaurus rex* (T. rex) roamed North America about 65 million years ago. For years, it was thought of as the king of meat-eating dinosaurs. It was a truly massive animal. It grew to 40 feet in length and weighed as much as 7 tons. Recently, however, a new dino has been discovered. Its name is *Giganotosaurus*. It may be the real "king" dinosaur.

The discovery occurred in Argentina. Scientists found the fossils of the new dinosaur in the southern part of the country. Judging by its skeleton, the Giganotosaurus appears to outweigh the T. rex by as many as 3 tons. It may have been over 45 feet in length. The Giganotosaurus is also an older dinosaur. It lived about 100 million years ago.

1 **The purpose of this passage is to**
Ⓐ amuse.
Ⓒ persuade.
Ⓑ inform.
Ⓓ sell a product.

2 **You can conclude from this passage that**
Ⓐ scientists will never discover a bigger dinosaur than the *Giganotosaurus*.
Ⓑ scientists have learned everything there is to know about the *Giganotosaurus*.
Ⓒ scientists are still learning important things about dinosaurs.
Ⓓ T. rex and the *Giganotosaurus* were about the same weight.

C.   No one had tried to break the window. It was simply an accident. Rosemary and Leslie were playing basketball in front of Rosemary's garage.

It wasn't that Rosemary wasn't a skilled basketball player. In fact, she was exceptionally talented. She had a superior jump shot. She could dribble equally well with both hands. She was accomplished at grabbing rebounds. The trouble was that she easily became distracted. In the middle of a game, she would see a neighbor's automobile drive by and instead of focusing on the game, she would wave. Sometimes, in the middle of a shot, she would begin thinking about what she wanted for dinner.

Anyway, after the game was finished, Leslie threw the ball to Rosemary. As usual, however, Rosemary was thinking about something else. The ball sailed straight past her and through the living-room window.

"Oh no!" shouted Leslie. "We have to go and explain to your parents."

"You're right," said Rosemary. "Let's find them before they come to us."

1 **How does Leslie seem to feel about the accident?**
Ⓐ thrilled
Ⓒ happy
Ⓑ upset
Ⓓ bored

2 **The next paragraph is likely to be about**
Ⓐ Rosemary's new neighbor.
Ⓑ Leslie's favorite activities.
Ⓒ how they learned to play basketball.
Ⓓ how Rosemary's parents react to the accident.

D. The Galápagos Islands are a special place. Located 600 miles from Ecuador's coast, they have all kinds of wildlife. About 5,000 species of plants and animals call the islands home. Many are unique. Animals like the Galápagos tortoise exist nowhere else in the world.

Sadly, some of these species are in danger. For example, the tortoise population has shrunk from 250,000 to about 25,000. The number of sea lions has shrunk, too. So has the number of birds.

There are many different reasons why this wildlife is threatened. One reason is tourism. Since the 1960s, people have flocked to the islands. They come to see tortoises, iguanas, and penguins.

Today, about 150,000 tourists arrive every year. The crowds put stress on the fragile habitat. Their boats bring insects and other pests. These pests can harm the islands' native species.

1 The main idea of this passage is that
Ⓐ the unique wildlife of the Galápagos is endangered.
Ⓑ insects can harm the islands' native species.
Ⓒ the Galápagos are located off Ecuador's coast.
Ⓓ tourists don't like animals.

2 Which of these is an *opinion*?
Ⓐ There are about 25,000 tortoises.
Ⓑ There were 250,000 tortoises.
Ⓒ The number of sea lions has shrunk.
Ⓓ The Galápagos are special.

E. Have you ever thought about taking a long bike trip? They can be a lot of fun. Keep in mind, however, that you'll need to bring along the proper equipment. Carrying the essentials can mean the difference between a great trip and a bad one.

The most important piece of equipment is a helmet, naturally. A helmet will help to keep you safe if an accident occurs. A good helmet should fit snugly onto your head. A helmet that fits improperly might not provide you with sufficient protection. Other important items are a spare inner tube, a compact pump, and a multi-tool set. If you're in a distant place when a tire goes flat or a spoke comes loose, you'll be happy to have brought these items along.

1 A helmet that doesn't fit properly
Ⓐ will usually protect the rider.
Ⓑ won't be as comfortable for the rider.
Ⓒ might not provide protection in an accident.
Ⓓ is an important piece of equipment.

2 The purpose of this passage is to
Ⓐ make you laugh at how funny bike trips are.
Ⓑ inform you about what to bring on a bike trip.
Ⓒ persuade you not to go on bike trips.
Ⓓ tell you a story about a bike trip.

Vocabulary

Synonyms

Read the underlined word in each phrase. Mark the word below it that has the same (or close to the same) meaning.

Sample:

sole survivor

- (A) only
- (B) lucky
- (C) large
- (D) silly

1 conceal the evidence
- (A) display
- (B) contribute
- (C) protect
- (D) hide

2 from another era
- (A) place
- (B) story
- (C) time period
- (D) community

3 beg to differ
- (A) gather
- (B) disagree
- (C) remain
- (D) be forgiven

4 cherish the moment
- (A) forget
- (B) detect
- (C) disgrace
- (D) treasure

5 hair-raising situation
- (A) terrifying
- (B) thrilling
- (C) hilarious
- (D) fast-moving

6 supreme confidence
- (A) absolute
- (B) little
- (C) surprising
- (D) inadequate

7 acquire knowledge
- (A) lose
- (B) gain
- (C) reject
- (D) reflect

Antonyms

Read the underlined word in each phrase. Mark the word below it that means the opposite or nearly the opposite.

Sample:

create chaos

- (A) chatter
- (B) noise
- (C) disturbance
- (D) order

1 a flimsy excuse
- (A) unbelievable
- (B) early
- (C) late
- (D) solid

2 oppose the motion
- (A) tighten
- (B) support
- (C) cease
- (D) oppress

3 considerable expense
- (A) costly
- (B) worthwhile
- (C) unfortunate
- (D) insignificant

4 appropriate action
- (A) fast
- (B) unsuitable
- (C) discouraging
- (D) brazen

5 vague idea
- (A) precise
- (B) vacant
- (C) unclear
- (D) uneven

6 betray the cause
- (A) disturb
- (B) believe
- (C) support
- (D) understand

7 unjustly accused
- (A) fairly
- (B) sadly
- (C) nearly
- (D) personally

Reading Skills Practice Test 7
Reading Comprehension

Read each passage. Then, fill in the circle that best completes each sentence or answers each question.

SAMPLE

Victoria Falls is the world's most amazing waterfall. It is almost a mile wide. Two countries share Victoria Falls: Zimbabwe and Zambia. At the falls, the Zambezi River flows over a cliff. Thirty million gallons of water pass by each minute. The drop is 350 feet. The falling water creates an enormous roar. People can hear the sound over 20 miles away.

1 What is the best title for this passage?
Ⓐ "Zimbabwe and Zambia"
Ⓑ "The Mighty Victoria Falls"
Ⓒ "Sounds People Hear"
Ⓓ "Waterfalls of the World"

2 Which of these is an *opinion*?
Ⓐ It is almost a mile wide.
Ⓑ Two countries share the falls.
Ⓒ Victoria Falls is the world's most amazing waterfall.
Ⓓ Thirty million gallons of water pass by each minute.

A. Technology has changed the way we walk in the woods. In the past, hikers carried compasses to avoid getting lost. Today, wilderness lovers are more likely to carry GPS devices.

GPS stands for *global positioning system*. It was an invention of the U.S. Department of Defense. The department launched 24 satellites into orbit. For years, only the military used these satellites. Now, of course, they're **available** to everyone.

The first GPS devices were tiny radios that communicated with satellites. Now, cell phones have GPS apps. They find your location and display it on a screen. A GPS device can tell you exactly where you are,

anywhere on Earth. The most amazing thing about them is their size and their accuracy. They are incredibly small but such a big help if you get lost in the woods.

1 The main purpose of this passage is to
Ⓐ persuade.   Ⓒ warn.
Ⓑ amuse.   Ⓓ inform.

2 In this passage, the word **available** means
Ⓐ automatic.   Ⓒ accessible.
Ⓑ free.   Ⓓ additional.

3 According to the passage, GPS devices have replaced
Ⓐ satellites.   Ⓒ phones.
Ⓑ compasses.   Ⓓ radios.

B.   Eight dollars a ticket? Ten dollars a ticket? Fourteen dollars a ticket? Everyone loves movies, but how much is too much when it comes to price? Going to see a film has become more expensive. In some cities, it can cost more than sixty dollars to take a family of four to the movies—if you include popcorn and soda.

People in the movie business say that the cost of a ticket is still **reasonable**. They argue that ticket prices reflect the growing costs of making films. A big Hollywood blockbuster can cost over $300 million. Actors' salaries and special effects make up a big part of that expense.

Audiences may grumble when they have to pay more, but it hasn't kept them from filling theaters.

1 In this passage, the word **reasonable** means
   Ⓐ fair.
   Ⓒ unjust.
   Ⓑ expensive.
   Ⓓ irregular.

2 According to people in the movie business, why are ticket prices rising?
   Ⓐ People are willing to pay any amount for a ticket.
   Ⓑ Films are more expensive to make.
   Ⓒ Actors don't earn very much money.
   Ⓓ All films include expensive special effects.

C.   Dinosaurs no longer walk the planet, but there's one animal that comes close. It's called the Komodo dragon, and it's the largest lizard in the world.

There are about 6,000 of these monster reptiles. They live on a few small islands in Indonesia. A full-grown dragon can weigh 250 pounds or more and reach 10 feet in length. To reach this size, it eats all kinds of animals. Rats, birds, deer, and even water buffalo are food for the Komodo dragon.

People who live on the islands try to stay out of the dragon's path. Sometimes, the lizard will attack humans.

Historians believe that these lizards inspired myths and folktales about fire-breathing dragons. While they don't really breathe fire, their bite is very poisonous. An animal that is bitten by a Komodo dragon almost always dies.

1 When fully grown, a Komodo dragon
   Ⓐ can breathe fire.
   Ⓑ will not eat a water buffalo.
   Ⓒ can weigh 250 pounds or more.
   Ⓓ will always attack humans.

2 The best title for this passage is
   Ⓐ "Indonesian Reptiles."
   Ⓑ "Indonesia's Komodo Dragons."
   Ⓒ "Dragons That Breathe Fire."
   Ⓓ "Dragon Myths and Legends."

D. It takes a special potato to make great fries. That's one thing America's top chefs agree on. These expert cooks know that there are all kinds of potatoes, and each kind is good for a specific purpose. Russet potatoes, for example, are great for baking. Red potatoes are best when boiled. White potatoes are tastiest in potato salad.

The chefs also agree that potatoes are very nutritious. Potatoes contain protein and many vitamins. A single potato provides 50 percent of the daily requirement for vitamin C. In fact, potatoes, like lemons, were once prized by sailors. Vitamin C prevents scurvy. On long ocean voyages, eating potatoes helped seafarers avoid getting the disease.

To get the most nutrients out of a potato, listen to the chefs. They say to cook potatoes with the skin on. Vitamins are lost when potatoes are peeled before cooking.

One thing the chefs can't agree on is where the best potatoes are grown. Some say Washington. Others say Idaho. Still others **maintain** that it is Wisconsin.

1 In this passage, the word **maintain** means
- Ⓐ know.
- Ⓒ repeat.
- Ⓑ argue.
- Ⓓ react.

2 According to the passage, sailors ate potatoes because
- Ⓐ potatoes help prevent a disease.
- Ⓑ potatoes taste delicious.
- Ⓒ potatoes contain protein.
- Ⓓ russet potatoes are great for baking.

E. Did you know that giant otters live in South America's Amazon region? These water-loving creatures can grow as long as six feet. They **prowl** the Amazon in packs. Banding together helps them hunt for fish and protect their babies from crocodiles.

Giant otters also speak their own unique language. Whistles, whines, squeals, and snorts are all part of the otter's vocabulary. Each sound means a different thing. If a giant otter thinks a human hunter is getting too close, it will snort "pffttt!" This sound warns other otters of danger.

Giant otters have to warn each other a lot. Because of hunting, it is estimated there are now only about 4,000 of these creatures left in the wild.

1 How do giant otters warn each other about hunters?
- Ⓐ They snort.
- Ⓒ They whistle.
- Ⓑ They squeal.
- Ⓓ They whine.

2 In this passage, the word **prowl** means
- Ⓐ live.
- Ⓒ move through.
- Ⓑ die.
- Ⓓ collect.

3 Why are there only about 4,000 giant otters left in the wild?
- Ⓐ The crocodiles have eaten many of them.
- Ⓑ Many of them have been killed by hunters.
- Ⓒ Their language is very hard to learn.
- Ⓓ The Amazon region is being polluted.

Vocabulary

Synonyms

Read the underlined word in each phrase. Mark the word below it that has the same (or close to the same) meaning.

Sample:

linger around
- (A) run
- (B) jump
- (C) look
- (D) wait

1 desert isle
- (A) aisle
- (B) island
- (C) lily
- (D) while

2 precise drawing
- (A) quick
- (B) accurate
- (C) humorous
- (D) bad

3 time to rejoice
- (A) relate
- (B) celebrate
- (C) examine
- (D) spend

4 weather forecast
- (A) screen
- (B) prediction
- (C) person
- (D) show

5 sincere remark
- (A) awful
- (B) friendly
- (C) unexpected
- (D) honest

6 fabulous recipe
- (A) excellent
- (B) tasteless
- (C) difficult
- (D) frivolous

7 humiliating event
- (A) successful
- (B) embarrassing
- (C) disturbing
- (D) frightening

Antonyms

Read the underlined word in each phrase. Mark the word below it that means the opposite or nearly the opposite.

Sample:

hard-working fellow
- (A) lazy
- (B) active
- (C) smart
- (D) humble

1 prehistoric cave
- (A) frightening
- (B) damp
- (C) ancient
- (D) modern

2 fragile instrument
- (A) heavy
- (B) dangerous
- (C) costly
- (D) unbreakable

3 captive prisoner
- (A) powerful
- (B) civil
- (C) disgraceful
- (D) escaped

4 attract flies
- (A) repel
- (B) swat
- (C) beckon
- (D) avoid

5 awful uproar
- (A) election
- (B) performance
- (C) flavor
- (D) silence

6 artificial flavoring
- (A) superficial
- (B) delicious
- (C) unusual
- (D) natural

7 overtake the leader
- (A) overwhelm
- (B) obstruct
- (C) fall behind
- (D) rejoin

Reading Skills Practice Test 8
Reading Comprehension

Read each passage. Then, fill in the circle that best completes each sentence or answers each question.

SAMPLE

When the *Titanic* sank, in 1912, the disaster became a hot topic for the entertainment industry. The first Titanic movie opened one month after the disaster. It starred Dorothy Gibson, an actress who had actually survived the disaster. And 85 years later, another *Titanic* movie was a **blockbuster**, wowing crowds everywhere.

1 This passage is mostly about
Ⓐ the sinking of the *Titanic*.
Ⓑ the building of the *Titanic*.
Ⓒ movies about the *Titanic*.
Ⓓ survivors of the *Titanic*.

2 In this passage, the word **blockbuster** means
Ⓐ failure.   Ⓒ wreck
Ⓑ success.   Ⓓ ship.

A.   Was your winter weather crazy this year? If so, the culprit may have been El Niño, a weather pattern that happens every three to seven years. The trouble starts in the Pacific Ocean when trade winds slow down. With less wind to blow the sun-warmed water away, normal cooling does not take place, and ocean temperatures rise. Warm water creates more moisture in the air, and so more rain falls in some places. This causes more rain to fall in many spots in North and South America. In addition, the changing winds push warm water away from Asia, Africa, and Australia. The resulting droughts that occur on these three continents can cause wildfires.

1 What is the best title for this passage?
Ⓐ "More Fish in the Ocean"
Ⓑ "Rain!"
Ⓒ "How El Niño Affects Weather"
Ⓓ "Weather Above the Pacific Ocean"

2 Which part of El Niño happens first?
Ⓐ Wildfires occur.
Ⓑ Ocean temperatures rise.
Ⓒ There is moisture in the air.
Ⓓ Rain hits North and South America.

3 How can El Niño cause fires?
Ⓐ The sun is hotter than usual.
Ⓑ Less rain in some areas causes a drought that can lead to fires.
Ⓒ The ocean water is warmer and can cause fires.
Ⓓ The ocean water disappears.

B. Carlos: Did you watch the basketball game last night?

Sam: Sure. I couldn't believe it when Carter went in for that dunk. It was amazing!

Carlos: I missed that part. How'd he do it?

Sam: Well, first he caught a pass from the point guard. Then, he dribbled towards the hoop. And then, he flew up from about five feet away and slammed the ball home.

Carlos: He's really an incredible player.

Sam: Yeah, I'll say. I wish I could dunk like that.

Carlos: Me, too. But coach says I'll have to grow a few inches first.

Sam: You and me both. I guess now we should get dressed and go to practice.

1 Which of these is a *fact*?

Ⓐ Carter is an incredible player.

Ⓑ Carter's dunk was amazing.

Ⓒ Carter slammed the ball home.

Ⓓ Carter's dunk was unbelievable.

2 During his dunk, which of the following did Carter do second?

Ⓐ caught a pass from the point guard

Ⓑ dribbled towards the hoop

Ⓒ took off from five feet away

Ⓓ slammed the ball home

3 How is Carter different from Carlos and Sam?

Ⓐ He's short.

Ⓑ He plays basketball.

Ⓒ He's a guy.

Ⓓ He can dunk well.

C. The Philippines is a beautiful country. This nation in Southeast Asia is made up of many islands. Its capital, Manila, is located on Luzon, the largest of the islands. In the north of Luzon, rice is grown in paddies. These rice paddies are unique and attract tourists from all over the world.

Other islands in the Philippines attract tourists as well. Palawan, the westernmost island, is popular with snorkelers and divers because it has beautiful coral reefs. Another popular Palawan tourist attraction is the Underground River, which runs through a cave. You can canoe down this river for over half a mile. You'll see enormous caves with one-hundred-foot ceilings, and giant stalagmites and stalactites. But this ride is not for the squeamish. All over the cave walls and ceilings, thousands of bats are sleeping—upside down!

1 Where is the Philippines located?

Ⓐ Northern Africa   Ⓒ Central Asia

Ⓑ Southeast Asia   Ⓓ Australia

2 The main purpose of this passage is to

Ⓐ inform.   Ⓒ persuade.

Ⓑ entertain.   Ⓓ amuse.

3 Which of these is an *opinion* about the Philippines?

Ⓐ It is made up of many islands.

Ⓑ It is a beautiful country.

Ⓒ Palawan is its westernmost island.

Ⓓ Palawan is popular with snorkelers.

D.   Have you ever heard of "rappelling"? This form of mountaineering involves attaching yourself to a rope and harness and descending a steep slope. Instead of climbing down with your hands and feet, you actually walk down the slope backwards. It's certainly a quick—and scary—way to get down a mountain. Or, in my case, a waterfall!

The first time I went rappelling was down a mountain waterfall. It was over 70 feet high, and the water rushed over it furiously. My guide clipped me into a harness, attached a safety rope, and sent me over the side of the torrent of water. At first, I was terrified and hung on for dear life. But, after a while, I realized that I wouldn't fall, so I relaxed and began to enjoy my descent. After all, few people can say they have walked on a waterfall!

1   From this passage, you might guess that
  Ⓐ the narrator hated rappelling.
  Ⓑ waterfalls have warm water.
  Ⓒ rappelling is quite easy to do.
  Ⓓ the author's guide was a rappeller.

2   This passage would probably be found in a
  Ⓐ sports magazine.   Ⓒ newspaper.
  Ⓑ poetry book.   Ⓓ textbook.

3   The next paragraph might talk about
  Ⓐ how waterfalls are created.
  Ⓑ the author's next rappelling experience.
  Ⓒ water pollution.
  Ⓓ walking backwards.

E.   Dr. James Harvey, wanted to find out if sea lions could be trained to use a video camera. He trained two sea lions named Beaver and Sake to use video cameras underwater. With the cameras strapped to their backs, the sea lions filmed gray whales diving off the coast of California. The video helped Harvey learn more about how the whales behave in the deep sea.

Harvey says humans can't dive deep enough to film the whales. Humans also sometimes scare the whales away. Sea lions are just right for the job because whales are not afraid of them.

Beaver and Sake practiced swimming near an **artificial** whale. They needed to stay close to the nose of the whale to get the best shots.

1   In this passage, the word **artificial** means
  Ⓐ fake.   Ⓒ lively.
  Ⓑ cute.   Ⓓ enormous.

2   The main idea of this passage is that
  Ⓐ sea lions can help scientists study gray whales.
  Ⓑ sea lions are cute and cuddly.
  Ⓒ gray whales are interesting animals.
  Ⓓ sea lions have to practice before using video cameras in the ocean.

3   You can guess from the passage that
  Ⓐ people want to learn about whales.
  Ⓑ sea lions are smarter than whales.
  Ⓒ people can't dive in the ocean.
  Ⓓ scientists don't have time to film whales.

Vocabulary

Which Word Is Missing?

In each of the following paragraphs, a word is missing. First, read each paragraph. Then, choose the missing word from the list beneath the paragraph. Fill in the circle next to the word that is missing.

Sample:

Jerome's dad belongs to the neighborhood safety association. Last night, it was his turn to _____ the block. He walked up and down all night, keeping everyone safe.

Ⓐ sweep   Ⓒ patrol
Ⓑ leave   Ⓓ study

❶ When airplanes were first _____ they were small and relatively slow. However, today's jets can go very fast. Some go faster than the speed of sound!

Ⓐ improved   Ⓒ searched
Ⓑ repaired   Ⓓ invented

❷ One thing that hasn't changed is the seriousness of a pilot's job. A pilot should never be _____. Doing careless or dangerous things risks lives.

Ⓐ reckless   Ⓒ energetic
Ⓑ accurate   Ⓓ strict

❸ Passengers are certainly more comfortable than they used to be. Old jet planes were very noisy. People used to wear earplugs to keep out the _____.

Ⓐ filth   Ⓒ din
Ⓑ music   Ⓓ moisture

❹ Airports have changed, too. Passengers used to walk onto the runway when getting on and off the plane. Now, upon _____, the plane parks at a gate that leads right inside the airport.

Ⓐ transportation   Ⓒ publication
Ⓑ landscape   Ⓓ arrival

❺ _____ handling has really improved as well. These days people wait a much shorter time to pick up their suitcases after a flight.

Ⓐ Security   Ⓒ Refund
Ⓑ Disturbance   Ⓓ Baggage

❻ Many people would say that having chocolate cake for _____ is a great treat. They can't think of a better way to end dinner.

Ⓐ lunch   Ⓒ dessert
Ⓑ delightful   Ⓓ menu

❼ It's rare that people will leave even a _____ of chocolate cake on their plates. They want to eat every bite.

Ⓐ morsel   Ⓒ mortal
Ⓑ meager   Ⓓ variety

Reading Skills Practice Test 9
Reading Comprehension

Read each passage. Then, fill in the circle that best completes each sentence or answers each question.

SAMPLE

Despite their danger to humans, rattlesnakes rarely kill each other. When two rattlers fight, they never deliver a deadly bite. Instead, they lift their heads and push each other. The snake that gets pushed to the ground slinks away. The instinct not to kill each other helps keep the species alive.

1 What is the best title for this passage?
Ⓐ "Endangered Snakes"
Ⓑ "Snakes of the World"
Ⓒ "How Rattlesnakes Fight"
Ⓓ "Rattlesnake Bites"

2 After a fight, a losing rattlesnake
Ⓐ bites the winner.
Ⓑ slinks away.
Ⓒ lifts its head.
Ⓓ dies.

A. Do you know how to make rice? First, measure out the exact amount of rice you need. Then, rinse the rice several times in cold water. Put it in a pot with exactly twice as much water as rice. Place the pot over medium heat and bring it to a boil. When it comes to a boil cover the pot tightly with a lid and turn the heat down very low. Let it cook for exactly 17 minutes. Don't peek! Then, turn off the heat and let the pot of rice stand for another 5 minutes. Finally, fluff it with a fork.

1 What is the best title for this passage?
Ⓐ "How to Cook Rice"
Ⓑ "Using the Stove"
Ⓒ "How to Serve Rice"
Ⓓ "Slow Cooking"

2 Right after you cover the pot with a lid, you should
Ⓐ rinse the rice.
Ⓑ turn down the heat.
Ⓒ add water.
Ⓓ fluff the rice with a fork.

3 The purpose of this passage is to
Ⓐ inform.   Ⓒ entertain.
Ⓑ persuade.   Ⓓ inspire.

B.   Scientists say houseplants do more than decorate homes and offices. They can also improve the quality of the air we breathe. Buildings today are often airtight and have plenty of insulation. This makes them energy-efficient, but it also makes it hard for fresh air to enter.

Many houseplants can "clean" the stale air trapped inside buildings. Plant leaves take in carbon dioxide gas from the air. In return, they give out clean oxygen. Plants also take other dangerous gases from the air. For instance, one type of daisy takes in benzene, a chemical found in gasoline. Spider plants take in carbon monoxide. So why not keep a lot of houseplants around? They just might help you breathe easier.

1   Spider plants take in
  Ⓐ oxygen.
  Ⓑ insulation.
  Ⓒ benzene.
  Ⓓ carbon monoxide.

2   Why can't fresh air enter many newer buildings?
  Ⓐ They do not have enough spider plants.
  Ⓑ They are airtight and have a lot of insulation.
  Ⓒ They are too full of oxygen.
  Ⓓ They have too many people.

C.   At 29,032 feet, the peak of Mount Everest is the highest place on Earth. It used to be a tough place to get to. Everest is set deep in the Himalayan Mountains. It sits on the border between Nepal and China. For centuries, people had to work hard just to reach the mountain, never mind climb it.

In 1953, Edmund Hillary and Tenzing Norgay became the first people to climb Mount Everest. Since then, thousands of others have tried to climb it. Many fail. But they still claim that the experience is unique and incredible.

Now some people are saying that Everest is too dangerous for most climbers. The facts back them up. Many Everest climbers die in the attempt. People are also saying that the environment of Everest can't support so many climbers. Climbers use up valuable natural resources, and they leave behind a lot of trash.

1   Why was Everest a tough place to get to?
  Ⓐ It sits on a border.
  Ⓑ It lies deep in the Himalayas.
  Ⓒ Its peak is the highest on Earth.
  Ⓓ People die climbing it.

2   Which of the following is an *opinion*?
  Ⓐ Many Everest climbers die trying to climb the mountain.
  Ⓑ Mount Everest is the highest place on Earth.
  Ⓒ Climbing Everest is an incredible experience.
  Ⓓ Everest sits on a border.

D.   Every summer, Alisia Orosco, went in and out of the hospital. But Alisia wasn't sick. While a student in a middle school in Abilene, Texas, Alisia delivered stuffed animals to young patients who needed a friend.

"My baby brother used to have to be in the hospital all the time, but he was happy because he had Winnie the Pooh," said Alisia. She realized other kids in the hospital could use some fuzzy friends, too.

Alisia and her older brother saved their allowances to buy 15 stuffed animals. They gave them to patients at nearby hospitals. The response was so good, Alisia continued saving. Eventually she visited three hospitals regularly with bags of donated toys. "I hope to help as many kids as I can," Alisia said. "It makes me happy to make them smile."

1   How did Alisia say she felt when she helped people?
   Ⓐ proud   Ⓒ tired
   Ⓑ sad   Ⓓ happy

2   What made Alisia first realize that kids in hospitals might like getting stuffed animals?
   Ⓐ She had to stay in the hospital herself.
   Ⓑ She saw that her baby brother liked having a stuffed Winnie the Pooh when he was in the hospital.
   Ⓒ Her older brother told her to donate her stuffed animals.
   Ⓓ She visited three hospitals regularly with bags of toys.

E.   Bolivia is a South American country that borders Peru, Chile, Argentina, Brazil, and Paraguay. It has a variety of landscapes. The north of Bolivia is mainly tropical rain forest. The Amazon River snakes through the steamy forest. Since there aren't many roads, people often travel through this area on riverboats. The forest is home to many kinds of wildlife, including toucans, jaguars, and capybaras, the world's largest rodents.

Bolivia's capital, La Paz, is in the snow-capped Andes mountains. At more than 12,000 feet, it is the highest capital in the world! Unlike the rainy, humid rain forest, this mountain area is extremely **arid**.

1   In this passage, the word **arid** means
   Ⓐ wet.   Ⓒ dry.
   Ⓑ hot.   Ⓓ cool.

2   Bolivia's capital is special because
   Ⓐ it's in the rain forest.
   Ⓑ it's in the Andes.
   Ⓒ it has capybaras.
   Ⓓ it's the highest capital in the world.

3   This passage will likely go on to talk about
   Ⓐ mountains.
   Ⓑ other places in South America.
   Ⓒ tropical birds.
   Ⓓ North America.

Vocabulary

Synonyms

Read the underlined word in each phrase.
Mark the word below it that has the same
(or close to the same) meaning.

Sample:
    <u>reluctant</u> to go
- (A) eager
- (B) hesitant
- (C) late
- (D) surprised

1 <u>bawling</u> infant
- (A) crying
- (B) playing
- (C) eating
- (D) sleeping

2 <u>shapeless</u> being
- (A) shapely
- (B) formless
- (C) square
- (D) strange

3 <u>flurry</u> of activity
- (A) burst
- (B) end
- (C) halt
- (D) lack

4 <u>frail</u> child
- (A) unfriendly
- (B) delicate
- (C) strong
- (D) feverish

5 <u>perilous</u> journey
- (A) long
- (B) uncomfortable
- (C) interesting
- (D) dangerous

6 <u>sole</u> survivor
- (A) first
- (B) only
- (C) last
- (D) oldest

7 feeling <u>uneasy</u>
- (A) unfit
- (B) difficult
- (C) disappointed
- (D) uncomfortable

Antonyms

Read the underlined word in each phrase.
Mark the word below it that means the
opposite or nearly the opposite.

Sample:
    <u>spectacular</u> event
- (A) amazing
- (B) joyful
- (C) tragic
- (D) ordinary

1 driving <u>recklessly</u>
- (A) cautiously
- (B) wildly
- (C) slowly
- (D) carelessly

2 <u>inferior</u> brand
- (A) exterior
- (B) popular
- (C) superior
- (D) expensive

3 <u>prolong</u> the class
- (A) lengthen
- (B) shorten
- (C) end
- (D) begin

4 feel <u>panic</u>
- (A) calm
- (B) upset
- (C) disgust
- (D) content

5 <u>amateur</u> athlete
- (A) gifted
- (B) competitive
- (C) professional
- (D) untalented

6 <u>solemn</u> occasion
- (A) frequent
- (B) rare
- (C) sorry
- (D) cheerful

7 <u>spare</u> part
- (A) needed
- (B) extra
- (C) loose
- (D) costly

Reading Skills Practice Test 10
Reading Comprehension

Read each passage. Then, fill in the circle that best completes each sentence or answers each question.

SAMPLE

At age 28, Los Angeles Lakers basketball star Shaquille "Shaq" O'Neal slam-dunked his education and scored. How? He graduated from Louisiana State University. The 7-foot, 1-inch player had dropped out of college to play basketball. At the time, he promised his mom that he would finish college. He kept his word and returned eight years later.

1 What did Shaq promise his mom?
Ⓐ that he would finish college
Ⓑ that he would return to college when he was 28
Ⓒ that he would become a great basketball player
Ⓓ that he would join the Lakers

2 How many years after dropping out of college did Shaq return?
Ⓐ 28   Ⓒ 1
Ⓑ 7   Ⓓ 8

A. In 1787, 55 delegates from 12 states gathered in Philadelphia to write the U.S. Constitution. Future president George Washington led the convention. Other famous attendees included James Madison, Benjamin Franklin, and Alexander Hamilton.

At that time, the U.S. was governed by the Articles of Confederation. This document had been adopted in 1781. The delegates did not think the Articles of Confederation set up a strong central government. They wanted to create a new law of the land. It took the delegates 16 weeks to **draft** our Constitution. It went into effect in 1789, after it was ratified by the states.

1 The Articles of Confederation functioned as the nation's governing document
Ⓐ until 1781.
Ⓑ after 1789.
Ⓒ for just 16 weeks.
Ⓓ before the Constitution was adopted.

2 In this passage, the word **draft** means
Ⓐ write.   Ⓒ abolish.
Ⓑ discard.   Ⓓ call to war.

B.   Since they first rescued Missy from an animal shelter when she was just four months old, Missy's owners knew she was a perfect dog. So, they wanted another one just like her!

The couple hired a team of scientists to clone, or make a copy of, Missy. If they had been successful, Missy's owners would have had the world's first cloned pet.

Missy's owners insisted that Missy had the perfect bark and growl. But the doctor in charge of the "Missyplicity" project warned that Missy's clone might be very different from Missy herself. "You're not getting your old pet back," the doctor said. "You're getting a new pet that has the same genes as the old one."

Genes determine how living things grow. But genes are only half of the story. The environment is also very important. So, living conditions could make Missy's clone different from Missy.

Missy died in 2002 before the cloning succeeded. But scientists did succeed in cloning a dog in 2005.

1   What could make Missy's clone different from Missy?
   Ⓐ her genes   Ⓒ her tail
   Ⓑ her environment   Ⓓ her bark

2   What's the best title for this passage?
   Ⓐ "Dogs, Dogs, Dogs"
   Ⓑ "How Our Genes Work"
   Ⓒ "Cloning Missy"
   Ⓓ "Why Mutts Make the Best Dogs"

C.   The world's tigers are roaring back to life. Tiger experts had once predicted the big cats would be nearly **extinct** by the year 2000. But in a recent report from the National Tiger Conservation Authority, conservationists, or people who save wildlife, agreed that the population of the largest member of the cat family appears to be on the rise.

Most tigers live in Asian nations, including Sumatra, Burma, India, and Thailand. In these countries, tigers have faced serious threats to their survival. Poachers, or people who kill wild animals and sell the body parts, hunted tigers for profit. Historically, many people in China have used tiger bones to make medicine for muscular aches and pains.

Now, many Asian countries are arresting poachers. And many Chinese people are trying to use alternatives to tiger bones for their medicines.

In the early 1970s, 50,000 to 70,000 tigers lived in Asia. Today, only a few thousand survive in the wild. But instead of falling even lower, the number is on the rise once again.

Now that's something to roar about!

1   Which is a *fact*?
   Ⓐ Tigers belong in the zoo.
   Ⓑ Most tigers live in Asian nations.
   Ⓒ Most tigers are scary.
   Ⓓ It's important to help save tigers.

2   In this passage, the word **extinct** means
   Ⓐ smelly   Ⓒ rising
   Ⓑ alive   Ⓓ dead

D. Kellie Vaughn was a poet but didn't know it—at least not until she was 12. Desperate for a Father's Day gift, she **penned** her first poem in honor of her dad.

"Before then, I hated to write anything," says the Huntsville, Alabama, native. "Poetry has taught me about myself and the world around me."

Now, Kellie is a prize-winning poet. She also started a poetry website just for children. Many kids send in poems about friendship, family, or school. Some of the poems rhyme, and some do not. Kellie believes any subject or form is fine. "It's about what flows from your mind," she says.

1 In this passage, the word **penned** means
   Ⓐ bought.   Ⓒ read.
   Ⓑ drew.   Ⓓ wrote.

2 Which is an *opinion*?
   Ⓐ Kellie Vaughn started a website for kids' poetry.
   Ⓑ Kellie has won prizes for her own poetry.
   Ⓒ It is hard to write poems.
   Ⓓ Poems do not all rhyme.

3 According to Kellie, poems should be about
   Ⓐ rainbows and flowers.
   Ⓑ what flows from your mind.
   Ⓒ your father or mother.
   Ⓓ the president of the United States.

E. In Bunol, Spain, the term "food fight" takes on a whole new meaning. Bunol is the site of an **annual** tomato fight, known as the Tomatina.

Each year, on the last Wednesday in August, the people of Bunol pelt each other with tomatoes. About 20,000 people take part. Many of them are kids. Over 240,000 pounds of tomatoes are thrown.

After the fight ends, the town is covered in tomato juice, pulp, and seeds. But the mess isn't left for someone else to take care of. The fighters who made the mess actually get together to clean it up.

They don't make tomato sauce with what remains on the streets of their town. They just return the streets to their original state.

1 How many tomatoes are used in the tomato fight?
   Ⓐ 20 pounds   Ⓒ 20,000 pounds
   Ⓑ 200 pounds   Ⓓ 240,000 pounds

2 In this passage, the word **annual** means
   Ⓐ large.   Ⓒ yearly.
   Ⓑ amazing.   Ⓓ monthly.

3 What is the best title for this passage?
   Ⓐ "A Real Food Fight"
   Ⓑ "All About Tomatoes"
   Ⓒ "Bunol—A Quiet Town"
   Ⓓ "Spanish Food"

Vocabulary

Synonyms

Read the underlined word in each phrase.
Mark the word below it that has the same
(or close to the same) meaning.

Sample:
>   departing flight
>   (A) long   (C) breaking
>   (B) flying   (D) leaving

1 absurd idea
(A) good   (C) interesting
(B) ridiculous (D) quick

2 tranquil seas
(A) wavy   (C) calm
(B) wet   (D) cold

3 menacing dog
(A) threatening (C) friendly
(B) furry   (D) large

4 diminish in number
(A) rise   (C) count
(B) list   (D) lessen

5 at dusk
(A) evening   (C) morning
(B) midnight   (D) noon

6 demand an answer
(A) desire   (C) require
(B) refuse   (D) offer

7 eerie noise
(A) loud   (C) creepy
(B) quiet   (D) cheerful

Antonyms

Read the underlined word in each phrase.
Mark the word below it that means the
opposite or nearly the opposite.

Sample:
>   dim room
>   (A) dark   (C) soft
>   (B) thick   (D) bright

1 purchase clothing
(A) shop   (C) take
(B) carry   (D) sell

2 acting ungrateful
(A) thankful   (C) rich
(B) poor   (D) spoiled

3 tardy arrival
(A) skinny   (C) early
(B) kind   (D) late

4 base of the building
(A) ball   (C) bat
(B) top   (D) bottom

5 stop the racket
(A) tennis   (C) silence
(B) cold   (D) din

6 modest improvement
(A) small   (C) false
(B) big   (D) temporary

7 unjust treatment
(A) unfair   (C) unkind
(B) fair   (D) lenient

Tested Skills	Item Numbers				
	Practice Test 1	Practice Test 2	Practice Test 3	Practice Test 4	Practice Test 5
Quote accurately from a text when explaining what the text says explicitly and when drawing inferences from the text.		B1, C2	A1, B2, C2, C3, D2, E1	A2, E1,	B1, C2, D1
Determine a theme of a story, drama, or poem from details in the text, including how characters in a story or drama respond to challenges or how the speaker in a poem reflects upon a topic; summarize the text.	A1, B1	A3	A3, B3	A1, C1	A1, E1
Compare and contrast two or more characters, settings, or events in a story or drama, drawing on specific details in the text.				C3	
Describe how a narrator's or speaker's point of view influences how events are described.		B2			
Determine two or more main ideas of a text and explain how they are supported by key details; summarize the text.	C1		E1,	B1	D2
Explain the relationships or interactions between two or more individuals, events, ideas, or concepts in a historical, scientific, or technical text based on specific information in the text.	A3, B2, B4, D1, E1, E2	A1, E2	D1	D2, E2	A3
Determine the meaning of general academic and domain-specific words and phrases in a text relevant to a grade 5 topic or subject area.	A2, B3, D1	A2, D2, E1	A2,	C2, D1	A2, C1
Draw on information from multiple print or digital sources, demonstrating the ability to locate an answer to a question quickly or to solve a problem efficiently.	C2	D1	B1, C1	B2	E2
Explain how an author uses reasons and evidence to support particular points in a text, identifying which reasons and evidence support which point(s).	C3			C4	B2
Know and apply grade-level phonics and word analysis skills in decoding words.		Synonyms 1–7, Antonyms 1–7	Synonyms 1–7, Antonyms 1–7	Synonyms 1–7, Antonyms 1–7	
Read grade-level text with purpose and understanding.	Which Word is Missing 1–5				Which Word is Missing 1–9
Use context to confirm or self-correct word recognition and understanding, rereading as necessary.	Which Word is Missing 1–5				Which Word is Missing 1–9
Determine or clarify the meaning of unknown and multiple-meaning words and phrases based on grade 5 reading and content, choosing flexibly from a range of strategies.	Which Word is Missing 1–5				Which Word is Missing 1–9
Use context as a clue to the meaning of a word or phrase.	Which Word is Missing 1–5	Synonyms 1–7, Antonyms 1–7	Synonyms 1–7, Antonyms 1–7	Synonyms 1–7, Antonyms 1–7	Which Word is Missing 1–9
Use the relationship between particular words to better understand each of the words.		Synonyms 1–7, Antonyms 1–7	Synonyms 1–7, Antonyms 1–7	Synonyms 1–7, Antonyms 1–7	

Tested Skills	Item Numbers				
	Practice Test 6	Practice Test 7	Practice Test 8	Practice Test 9	Practice Test 10
Quote accurately from a text when explaining what the text says explicitly and when drawing inferences from the text.	A1, A2, C2, E1,	A3, C1	B2, C1, D1, D3, E3	B1, C1, D1, E2, E3	A1, D3, E1
Determine a theme of a story, drama, or poem from details in the text, including how characters in a story or drama respond to challenges or how the speaker in a poem reflects upon a topic; summarize the text.		A1, C2	A1, C2, E2	A1	B2, E3
Compare and contrast two or more characters, settings, or events in a story or drama, drawing on specific details in the text.			A3, B3	B2, D2	B1
Describe how a narrator's or speaker's point of view influences how events are described.	C1				
Determine two or more main ideas of a text and explain how they are supported by key details; summarize the text.	D1				
Explain the relationships or interactions between two or more individuals, events, ideas, or concepts in a historical, scientific, or technical text based on specific information in the text.	B2	B2, D2, E1, E3	A2	A2	
Determine the meaning of general academic and domain-specific words and phrases in a text relevant to a grade 5 topic or subject area.		A2, B1, D1, E2	E1	E1	A2, C2, D1, E2
Draw on information from multiple print or digital sources, demonstrating the ability to locate an answer to a question quickly or to solve a problem efficiently.	D2		B1, C3	C2	C1, D2
Explain how an author uses reasons and evidence to support particular points in a text, identifying which reasons and evidence support which point(s).	B1, E2		D2	A3	
Know and apply grade-level phonics and word analysis skills in decoding words.	Synonyms 1–7, Antonyms 1–7	Synonyms 1–7, Antonyms 1–7		Synonyms 1–7, Antonyms 1–7	Synonyms 1–7, Antonyms 1–7
Read grade-level text with purpose and understanding.			Which Word is Missing 1–7		
Use context to confirm or self-correct word recognition and understanding, rereading as necessary.			Which Word is Missing 1–7		
Determine or clarify the meaning of unknown and multiple-meaning words and phrases based on grade 5 reading and content, choosing flexibly from a range of strategies.			Which Word is Missing 1–7		
Use context as a clue to the meaning of a word or phrase.	Synonyms 1–7, Antonyms 1–7	Synonyms 1–7, Antonyms 1–7	Which Word is Missing 1–7	Synonyms 1–7, Antonyms 1–7	Synonyms 1–7, Antonyms 1–7
Use the relationship between particular words to better understand each of the words.	Synonyms 1–7, Antonyms 1–7	Synonyms 1–7, Antonyms 1–7		Synonyms 1–7, Antonyms 1–7	Synonyms 1–7, Antonyms 1–7

ANSWER KEY

Practice Test 1
Reading Comprehension
Sample: **1.** A **2.** C
A: 1. B **2.** D **3.** D
B: 1. A **2.** D **3.** A **4.** C
C: 1. C **2.** B **3.** D
D: 1. D **2.** A
E: 1. A **2.** B

Vocabulary
Which Word Is Missing?, Sample: B
1. D **2.** C **3.** B **4.** A **5.** B

Practice Test 2
Reading Comprehension
Sample: **1.** B
A: 1. A **2.** D **3.** B
B: 1. B **2.** B
C: 1. B **2.** D
D: 1. A **2.** B
E: 1. A **2.** B

Vocabulary
Synonyms, Sample: B
1. A **2.** C **3.** B **4.** D **5.** A **6.** B **7.** B
Antonyms, Sample: C
1. A **2.** D **3.** D **4.** A **5.** C **6.** D **7.** D

Practice Test 3
Reading Comprehension
Sample: **1.** D **2.** B
A: 1. B **2.** A **3.** B
B: 1. C **2.** B **3.** B
C: 1. D **2.** B **3.** B
D: 1. A **2.** D
E: 1. A **2.** D

Vocabulary
Synonyms, Sample: D
1. C **2.** C **3.** A **4.** C **5.** D **6.** C **7.** C
Antonyms, Sample: B
1. A **2.** B **3.** D **4.** C **5.** A **6.** B **7.** C

Practice Test 4
Reading Comprehension
Sample: **1.** A **2.** C
A: 1. D **2.** A
B: 1. A **2.** C
C: 1. A **2.** D **3.** C **4.** C
D: 1. D **2.** A
E: 1. C **2.** C

Vocabulary
Synonyms, Sample: C
1. A **2.** C **3.** B **4.** A **5.** B **6.** A **7.** B
Antonyms, Sample: B
1. B **2.** C **3.** D **4.** A **5.** D **6.** C **7.**C

Practice Test 5
Reading Comprehension
Sample: **1.** C **2.** D
A: 1. B **2.** C **3.** A
B: 1. B **3.** A
C: 1. A **2.** B
D: 1. D **2.** D
E: 1. A **2.** C

Vocabulary
Which Word Is Missing?, Sample: B
1. D **2.** A **3.** C **4.** D **5.** A
6. B **7.** A **8.** D **9.** C

Practice Test 6
Reading Comprehension
Sample: **1.** B **2.** A
A: 1. D **2.** D
B: 1. B **2.** C
C: 1. B **2.** D
D: 1. A **2.** D
E: 1. C **2.** B

Vocabulary
Synonyms, Sample: A
1. D **2.** C **3.** B **4.** D **5.** A **6.** A **7.** B
Antonyms, Sample: D
1. D **2.** B **3.** D **4.** B **5.** A **6.** C **7.** A

ANSWER KEY

Practice Test 7
Reading Comprehension
Sample: **1.** B **2.** C
A: 1. D **2.** C **3.** B
B: 1. A **2.** B
C: 1. C **2.** D
D: 1. B **2.** A
E: 1. A **2.** C **3.** B

Vocabulary
Synonyms, Sample: D
1. B **2.** B **3.** B **4.** B **5.** D **6.** A **7.** B
Antonyms, Sample: A
1. D **2.** D **3.** D **4.** A **5.** D **6.** D **7.** C

Practice Test 8
Reading Comprehension
Sample: **1.** C **2.** B
A: 1. C **2.** B **3.** B
B: 1. C **2.** B **3.** D
C: 1. B **2.** A **3.** B
D: 1. D **2.** A **3.** B
E: 1. A **2.** A **3.** A

Vocabulary
Which Word Is Missing?, Sample: C
1. D **2.** A **3.** C **4.** D **5.** D **6.** C **7.** A

Practice Test 9
Reading Comprehension
Sample: **1.** C **2.** B
A: 1. A **2.** B **3.** A
B: 1. D **2.** B
C: 1. B **2.** C
D: 1. D **2.** B
E: 1. C **2.** D **3.** B

Vocabulary
Synonyms, Sample: B
1. A **2.** B **3.** A **4.** B **5.** D **6.** B **7.** D
Antonyms, Sample: D
1. A **2.** C **3.** B **4.** A **5.** C **6.** D **7.** A

Practice Test 10
Reading Comprehension
Sample: **1.** A **2.** D
A: 1. D **2.** A
B: 1. B **2.** C
C: 1. B **2.** D
D: 1. D **2.** C **3.** B
E: 1. D **2.** C **3.** A

Vocabulary
Synonyms, Sample: D
1. B **2.** C **3.** A **4.** D **5.** A **6.** C **7.** C
Antonyms, Sample: D
1. D **2.** A **3.** C **4.** B **5.** C **6.** B **7.** B